Books published by 410-HOPE Publishing are available at special
discount for bulk purchases in the United States for corporations,
institutes, and other organizations. For more information, please
contact me at thehiphoplectures@gmail.com

Text set in 13.5-point Arial Narrow
Includes bibliographical references and Index

A CIP catalog record for this book is available from the Library of
Congress.

ISBN: 10: 0986104124

ISBN: 13: 978-0-9861041-2-1 (Printed Version)

Acknowledgements

This book is dedicated to a couple of people starting with Patricia (Mom aka "Love" aka Ma' Pat), Kimberly (Big Little Sister aka "Faith" aka Keezy), and DeLena (Linka aka Bestie aka Right-hand).

This book is dedicated to my family and those who became my family, which includes Grandma (aka Mattie), Grandpa, Ms. Twiggy, Erin, Tiffany, Nyasha (aka Nynia), Ms. Sonya, Ms. Nancy, Ms. Sandra, Kamila, Swapna, Aunt Holly, Aunt Shirley, Uncle Ricky, Dr. Roseboro, Tahmar, and anyone with "a dollar and a dream."

This book is dedicated to my co-workers and students from Dance 147 (aka Hip Hop History Lecture Class), since 2006.

Last, but not least this book is dedicated to GOD!

The Hip Hop Lectures

(Volume 2)

By:

Dr. T.L. Osborne

Table of Contents

Introduction: Why Am I Writing This Book?

There are many aspects of Hip Hop culture that exceeds beyond just the beat, a dance, or a catchy hook. *The Hip Hop Lectures* (*Volume 2*) is a book that was created to make a connection between the past and the present, as it relates to Hip Hop culture. Hip Hop culture has been able to accomplish so much in such a very short period of time, most of which includes the bridging of generational and racial gaps locally and internationally. The hope; however, is that the culture continues to grow and evolve to a point where decades and centuries later, people will still be talking about some of the pioneers and innovators of such a wonderful musically inspired movement. *The Hip Hop Lectures* (*Volume 2*) is not the know-it-all of the Hip Hop culture or any culture, but an honest attempt to provide insight about how the past affects the present and future. *The Hip Hop Lectures* (*Volume 2*) is inspired by actual lectures used to teach anyone who has an interest in Hip Hop culture, beyond just music.

Discussing the connections between Hip Hop culture and history is significant. The fact that Hip Hop culture's history derives from the continent of Africa and currently expands throughout the world is nothing shorter than amazing. Each topic mentioned in this book could have its own volume of work; however, the content expressed is condensed in a way to provide the reader with basic historical information and encourage personal reflection and research. Understanding the historical connection between Hip Hop and history, allows one to realize how the youth of an enslaved culture have managed to create a world-wide multi-billionaire phenomenon known as Hip Hop culture. For anyone to come from "Nothing into something" is inspirational. After reading this book, my sincerest hope is that anyone who reads this book will be able to appreciate Hip Hop culture and see the culture's value on an educational level; in

spite of the good, bad, and indifferent sides of the culture.

Thank you for picking this book to read. I "HOPE" you enjoy

reading my life's passion.

Chapter 1

Hip Hop Culture: The Evolution

If the history of Hip Hop culture could be defined into a few words, these words would be "coming from nothing into something." Hip Hop culture has a rag to riches story of success. Early contributors, innovators, participants, and aficionados of Hip Hop culture never realized that the culture would be as influential and impactful locally and globally. Young, poor, talented, and urban kids innovatively created a multi-billion dollar industry. Who knew that two record players could be joined together with a few wire connections to create a best of both worlds sound? Who knew that Adidas track suits and sneakers could be fashionable? Who knew that breakdancing on a cardboard box could eventually lead you to dancing on stage and television shows in front of millions of people?

On the 1996 *Life After Death* album; the Notorious B.I.G. coined what would become the goal for his life and anyone else's life who desires to become successful. The phrase for success, in Hip Hop culture, is "going from ashy to classy." Most rap artists talk about what life was like before the fame, which reflects the same sentiments that Notorious B.I.G. expressed in 1996. Some examples are present in 50 Cent's song, *Window Shopper,* Kanye West's song *Good Life (2007)*, Lupe Fiasco's song, *Hood Now/Outro* (2012), and Nicki Minaj's song, *I'm the Best* (2012):

50 cents' Verse

You's a window shopper/ Mad at me, I think I know why.../
In the jewelry store lookin' at sh** you can't buy/
In the dealership tryin' to get a test drive.../
Mad as f*** when you see me ride by

Kanye's Verse

Have you ever popped champagne on a plane,/ While gettin some brain…/ Whether you broke or rich, you gotta hit this/ Havin' money's not everything; not havin' it is…/ I always had a passion for flashin' Befo' I had it/ I closed my eyes and imagine/ The good life

Lupe Fiasco's Verse

That's right/ You in the hood now/ Ramen noodle soups, you make the best/ Water in the milk to make it stretch/ That's the hood now

Nicki Minaj's Verse

I remember when I couldn't buy my mother a couch/ Now I'm sitting at the closing, bought my mother a house…/ Cause even when my daddy was on crack I was crack/ Now, the whole album crack you ain't gotta skip a track/

These rap verses by 50 Cent, Kanye West, Lupe Fiasco, and Nicki Minaj are reflective of artists' experiences, struggles, and articulations about life before success and life after success. These sample verses from each artist allows the listeners to understand that before the hard work garnered fame, there was an enormous amount of growing pains.

Hip Hop culture started from humble beginnings and innocent activities, such as dj'ing, graffiti, breakdancing, and mc'ing; and an occasional mention of beatboxing. Hip Hop culture served as the alternative for gang affiliations and illegal activities. Because the Hip Hop movement initially started with young impoverished teenagers, who sought to be creative and have fun, in spite of the circumstances, the culture was able to experience steady growth, rather than a culture that had instantaneous and momentary success. In other words, Hip Hop culture was overlooked before being mass produced into a multi-billion dollar worldwide industry.

Element 1

History- Hip Hop culture's history dates back to Africa and includes various historical eras of influences dating back from slavery to Hip Hop culture's birth in New York. Jewelry, fashion, dance, drumbeats, and other notable aspects of Hip Hop cultural have roots in African cultural traditions. Therefore, understanding history becomes just as important as understanding Hip Hop culture currently.

Element 2

Language/Slang- Hip Hop culture's vernacular has always been a uniquely identifying characteristic of the culture. However, roots of language and slang were birthed during the days of slavery, when slaves spoke in broken dialect (ebonics) and began to emerge consistently during the Harlem Renaissance (1920s). During the Harlem Renaissance era, to be "Hip" was to be cool, down, or knowledgeable and "Hop" was often associated with dance, movement, and partying. Being able to develop acronyms, re-define words, and create new words is a constant part of the culture. Examples include, but are not limited to "fresh, grill, bling, wipe me down, dope, shizzle, skeet skeet, yo-lo, swag, kush, murk, brain, t.h.o.t., dab, fleek, b.a.e., turn-up, doe/bands/cake/paper/cheese, kick rocks, turn-up," and many more.

Element 3

Sampling/Stealing- Sampling is a unique term that can often allude to stealing. The terms could be used interchangeably; especially considering the history of music, musicians rights, as well as the impact that sampling and stealing has on determining who is the originator of certain style trends, songs, dances, styles, and entertainment trends. There is an old African proverb, "There is no original song, except the first song." Some would believe that sampling/stealing has been going on since the beginning of time; especially, once Africans arrived in America, during the slave trade. Several distinct periods of history reveal the level of sampling and thievery; especially during the Minstrel Show era (Thomas D. Rice), Harlem Renaissance era (black authors publishing works under pseudonyms or white authors), the Rock-N-Roll era (Elvis Presley), or even with the ascription of twerking to Miley Cyrus. Unfortunately, sampling/stealing did not become officially illegal until Elvis Presley, in 1961, sued James Tenney (*Collage No. 1, 1965)* for illegally sampling/ stealing the song, *Blue Suede Shoes.* Prior to this case, sampling/stealing was not a legal dispute that could be argued or proven in a court of law.

Sampling/Stealing is a unique topic in Hip Hop, because the culture includes elements from various genres and historical periods, which raises some questions about how authentic and creative Hip Hop culture can be if the culture constantly samples music legally and illegally sometimes. Producers, like Sean Combs, of the Bad Boy Record Label, was one of the premier producers who were able to capitalize on sampling/stealing without legal incidence in the 1990s, because many older artists were unaware of what Hip Hop culture was and that the songs were being sampled/stolen, because the older generations did not listen to rap. Today, one can find current incidents arising with rap artists illegally sampling/stealing music, because many artists (specifically older artists) do not want their music to be affiliated with rap music, because of the negative imagery and misogynistic lyrical content.

Element 4

Graffiti- Hip Hop culture's use of graffiti has always been

unique; however, so has the use of hieroglyphics, which are

present in mummy tombs, ancient murals, and on the encased

caskets of the dead throughout Africa (specifically in ancient

Egypt). Therefore, there is no wonder that graffiti becomes an

essential element of Hip Hop culture in terms of expression and

reflection, story-telling, branding, displaying societal awareness,

creating fashion trends. In other words, graffiti is one of the many

elements of Hip Hop that requires natural skills and artistry.

Graffiti is as multi-dimensional and multi-ethnic in essence. Most

graffiti artists uniquely developed his or her craft by: creating

flyers for local parties, creating clothing trends, telling stories on

self-made murals about communal or global issues or tragedies,

creating an awareness about social, economic, or political issues,

warning people about violence, or encouraging people to remain hopeful. Even though graffiti is a unique element of Hip Hop culture, initially this element of Hip Hop culture was not well received or perceived as a beneficial gift by larger society. Graffiti and graffiti artists were considered a public nuisance for the constant vandalism (defacing public property); especially in New York City, around 1970's.

Element 5

Dj'ing- Hip Hop culture's Dj's are considered the back-bone of the culture and beginning in the 1970's, specifically 1972 with the emergence of Dj Kool Herc and the evolution of the craft to include Grandwizard Theodore, Afrika Bambaataa, Grandmaster Flash, and other notable dj's like Kid Capri, Spinderella, Funkmaster Flex, Nick Cannon, and Dj Khalid. Clive Campbell (also known as Dj Kool Herc) was originally born in Kingston, Jamaica and raised in the Bronx (NY) is a founding Dj in Hip Hop culture. Kool Herc is responsible for introducing and popularizing key elements to dj'ing, which include bass sounds, break-beats, merry-go-rounds, and toasting.

- *Bass sounds*- described and synonymous with today's music (and associated specifically locations like Miami). This sound is often described as a speaker busting or heart pounding and throbbing type of sound, when heard through speakers.

- *Break-beats*- described as the part of the album when the lyrical content stops and only instruments are played. This is also described as being the best part of a song to dance on and is equivalent to the hook of a song.

- *Merry-go-rounds*- described as a technique that includes the connecting of multiple songs with other songs. The technique would begin with the Dj playing the best parts of a song and then connecting/ blending that best part of the song with another song's best part and so on. The purpose of this technique, the merry-go-round was so that audiences can dance all night long (24/7).

- *Toasting*- rooted in African tradition and equivalent to the call-and response technique. Toasting is referred as talking on the microphone and is similar to what a MC (master of ceremonies) would do at an event. This technique eventually would evolve beyond talking on a microphone and lead to people rapping on the microphone.

Dj Kool Herc was one of the pioneering and influential Dj's in Hip Hop culture and these four elements were key to the evolution of the art form. Unique aspects of Hip Hop culture includes the ability to innovate, but also to evolve. The impact that Dj Kool Herc had on Hip Hop culture with the inclusion of these four elements influenced other Dj's like Grandwizard Theodore, Afrika Bambaataa, and Grandmaster Flash.

Grandwizard Theodore (birth name Theodore Livingston) was born in Bronx, New York. Grandwizard Theodore started dj'ing at a young age and by the time he was a teenager, he perfected a dj'ing technique called needle-dropping. The technique is simplistic in name, but difficult in action. The process involves a complex ability to drop the needle of a record player onto an album at the exact point (normally on the breakbeat) consistently without having to cue up the album. Cueing is a technique that involves the process of having an exact part of the same album or another album waiting to play. Because needle dropping does not require cueing or additional equipment to find the same point on an album, the Dj can create faster movements as the album plays. Eventually, Grandmaster Flash would evolve Grandwizard Theodore's needle dropping technique by introducing and popularizing the dj'ing technique known into a new form of dj'ing, which would become known as scratching. The scratching technique (which is synonymous with Grandmaster Flash's brand) involves the possible use of a crossfader or mixer, while moving an album back and forth as the song plays.

Afrika Bambaataa (birth name Kevin Donovan) was born in Bronx, New York. Kevin Donovan was smart and talented at a young age. Because gangs were becoming prominent and dangerous for anyone who was not a member of a gang, Bambaataa joined a gang called The Black Spades in New York. Even though Kevin was a gang member, he still attended school, received good grades, and participated in school activities. During one of the school's semesters, teachers organized and sponsored an essay competition for the students. The students who won the essay content would win a trip to Africa. Kevin

Donovan won the essay contest to Africa and learned much more than he had anticipated. Kevin learned about the power of Zulu warriors and how destructive black-on-black violence can be to a community and future generations. Because of his trip to Africa and his newfound knowledge, Kevin Donovan returned home to New York and renamed himself Afrika Bambaataa. Bambaataa's inspiration while visiting Africa, led him to convince some of the Black Spade gang members to change their lives and become an empowering gang instead of a violent gang that aided in the destruction of their communities and future generations. Afrika Bambaataa would re-invent The Black Spades Gang into a Hip Hop crew, called Zulu Nation. What made the Zulu Nation special was more than just the transformation of the gang into a Hip Hop crew, but that fact that Zulu Nation was one of the premier crews in Hip Hop. Zulu Nation was one of the only crews, in New York, that included four of the founding Hip Hop elements: graffiti artists, dj's, breakdancers, and mc's. While at parties,

Bambaataa could easily assemble his crew and enter into every

competition/battle. As a result, Bambaataa even evolved his

dj'ing technique and introduced an electro/techno sound of music.

The 1982, song, *Planet Rock*, would become a foundational

record for Afrika Bambaataa's career.

Grandmaster Flash (birth name Joseph Saddler) was born

in Bridgetown, Barbados, but raised in the Bronx (NY).

Grandmaster Flash introduced the swagger and style to dj'ing.

Flash re-invigorates the dj'ing techniques such as scratching,

inventing cutting and mixing, as well fusing his dj'ing style

alongside a rap group known as the Furious Five. The

combination of Grandmaster Flash's techniques and these

rappers created a monumental blend of the Dj and rapper(s). The

group created what many Hip Hop enthusiast consider the

foundational song of Hip Hop culture. The song is called *The Message* (1982).

Each of the leading Dj's mentioned (Herc, Theodore, Bambaataa, and Flash) has made foundational contributions to Hip Hop culture history and evolved traditional dj'ing techniques making them legendary. What is even more interesting is that the majority of these Dj's have roots and connections to islands, like Jamaica and the continent of Africa, which creates a transatlantic sound to the music.

Element 6

Breakdancing- Breakdancing was popularized around 1976; the dance trend is practiced by many different ethnic groups; however, Puerto Ricans and Blacks lead the way with this particular dance trend. The Breakdancers favorite part of the album played by the Dj would be the break-beat, which would ignite dancers to begin to do various styles of breakdancing techniques. Breakdancing techniques included up-rock, top rock, down-rock, power moves, freezes, blow-up, flavor, spinning, popping, locking, strutting. Examples of original breakdancing legends would include the Rock Steady Crew (specifically Richard "Crazy Legs" Colon and Santiago "Jo Jo" Torres), Zulu Nation, as well as new-age groups like the Jabba Walkies. Breakdancing has gone from a street oriented culture to becoming a world-wide phenomenon and currently includes competitive exhibitions displayed on television shows like America's Best Dance Crews (ABDC), So You Think You Can Dance, Battle of the Year (BOTY), The Notorious IBE, Chelles Battle Pro, Red Bull BC One, Floor Wars, R16 Korea, and World B-Boy Classics.

Element 7

Mc'ing- Hip Hop culture's Mc's are an essential element

because the mc's foundationally provided a lyrical description of

reality for society (locally and globally). The mc can best be

described as the un-biased and truthful news reporter for a

community of people that have been stereotyped and forgotten.

In addition, the mc, historically, becomes relevant, to Hip Hop

culture, in two distinct years 1976 and 1977. Kurtis Blow (critically

acclaimed hit 1980 song, *The Breaks*) becomes the first

commercially successful solo rapper in 1976. In 1977, The Sugar

Hill Gang (*Rappers Delight*, 1979 song, sampled song from Chic's

Good Times) becomes the first commercially successful rap

group.

What are equally notable facts about these two distinct

artists are the names; "Blow," "Sugar," "Hill," as well as, "Gang."

The drug, crack cocaine, plays a pivotal role in Hip Hop culture;

especially in regards to the rapper, who serves as the communal storyteller. Therefore, there should not be a surprise to learn that rappers names have become intertwined with the drug culture. Rappers have chosen rap monikers that reference nicknames for drugs, drug paraphernalia, gangs, or drug dealer's and Kingpin names. What is also interesting is how many fake mc's would begin to emerge in Hip Hop culture (at this particular period in time) claiming to be authentic, but appearing to only capitalist of the culture? The Sugar Hill Gang is credited with being the first commercially successful rap group. However, the group's history is marred by thievery from one of the original influences in Hip Hop culture; Grandmaster/Dj Caz (who was a neighbor of Dj Kool Herc and was one of the first to serve simultaneously as a dj and mc, in Hip Hop culture). Sylvia Robinson created the group The Sugar Hill Gang and included three members: Wonder Mike, Big Bank Hank, Master Gee. Coincidentally, Big Bank Hank was a close friend and bouncer at a club, where Grandmaster/Dj Caz often performed. Because the group was created with the sole purpose of capitalizing financially on the newly popularized element known as rap, questions about an artist's actual talent and lyrical authenticity was over-looked, ignored, and considered irrelevant. Therefore, when the time came to prepare and record a verse for the groups' new single, *Rappers Delight*, Big Bank Hank relied on the recent and popularized verse he heard Grandmaster/Dj Caz rhyme weeks prior at the club. After recording the verse, Big Bank Hank, allegedly, visited Grandmaster/Dj Caz explaining how he used Caz's rap verse on a new song, while simultaneously asking Caz for permission to use additional rap verses written in Caz's book of rhymes. Should Caz allow Hank to use his rap verses, Hank promised to pay Caz for use of his lyrics, as well as arrange an opportunity for Caz to get a record deal. Grandmaster/Dj Caz agreed and unfortunately

Caz never retrieved any money, received any acknowledgement or accolades for his rap verses, or received an opportunity to get a record deal. The Sugar Hill Gang serves as an example of how an artists can rise to success commercially, but fail to succeed in the eyes of those from which Hip Hop culture was birthed; the underground

Element 8

Beatboxing- Beatboxing's connection to Hip Hop culture's history is another relevant element because of the creativity associated with the craft. Beatboxing coincidently becomes another creative form of Hip Hop culture, because most aspiring rap artists and beat-makers could not initially afford the equipment to make the sounds that he or she wanted and people. Also, rappers and beat-makers would eventually get tired of sacrificing their fists and wrists to bang on a table just so that rappers could have a beat to rhyme/freestyle over. Therefore, beatboxing became a free and in-expensive way to make beats. Beatboxing begins around the 1980s and includes many notable artists who pioneered or evolved the beatboxing craft includes: Rahzel (*If Your Mother Only Knew, 2000)*, Doug E Fresh featuring Dj Kool Herc (*Clear My Throat, 1996)*, Biz Markie (*Just a Friend, 2002)*, Will Smith (The Fresh Prince of Bel Air), The Fat Boys (*Human Beatbox, 1984)*, and even movie actors like Michael Winslow (*Police Academy* Movie Collection*)* revealed various skill levels to the craft. Even more interesting, is that most rappers have the ability to rap and beat-box as well, which most likely helped maintain a constant beat for rappers that was not contingent on one person. In other words, if a person did a beat for you to rhyme over reciprocate the favor by duplicating a beat for the next rapper.

Element 9

Beefs & Battle Rap Competitions- Competition is an important aspect of any aspect of life that seeks to separate the talented from the talent-less, those that can from those who cannot, those who are real from those who are fake, those who should be revered and those who should be abhorred. Beefs and battle rap competitions have become an important part of Hip Hop culture, because beefs and battle rap competitions provide entertainment for audiences, while simultaneously revealing an artist's level of acuity, creativeness, and cleverness. Beefs and battle rap competitions have also inspired artists, specifically rap artists, to rhyme some of the most creative and paramount lyrics one has ever heard. Beefs and battle raps competition also prove to be beneficial financially and promotionally for an artists' career. Beefs and battle rap competitions provide artists with an opportunity to become relevant instantaneously, while simultaneously gaining a stronger fan-base, and increasing popularity; all of which can pay off financially through record sales. In spite of the benefits that beefs and battle rap competitions can provide for an artists' career, engaging in a beef or battle rap competition (momentarily or continuously) can also create high levels of stress, paranoia, ignite violence, and either make or break an artist's career. The impact of beefs and battle rap competitions can be even more detrimental to the rap artists participating in a beef or battle rap competition because in one instance a rappers career can be destroyed or never be allowed to ascend. For example, an up-and-coming artist may want to bypass their amateur status, by calling out/challenging another popular rapper/top rapper. If the up-and-coming artist is successful, he or she can possibly de-throne and end the career of a notable elite rapper. However, if that up-and-coming artist fails to win the beef, then that particular artist's career may become obsolete before even starting a rap career. Hip Hop beefs began to emerge at two distinct periods: in, 1981, at a club between Kool Moe Dee and Busy Bee (which occurred spontaneously), while the more notable beef that introduced "beefing on wax" occurred in, 1984, between U.T.F.O. (Un.Touchable.Force.Organization.) and Roxanne Shante', based on a song called, *Roxanne' Roxanne'*. An embarrassing rap beef or battle competition can become a permanent scar over the victim and victor's rap legacies. Other notable beefs and battle rap competitions, for further research purposes, include the following:

- MC Shan (Queens Bridge) versus Krs-One (South Bronx)- 1985
- Mc Lyte vs. Antoinette- 1987
- Rakim vs. Big Daddy Kane- 1988

- Ice Cube vs. N.W.A.- 1989

- Biggie vs. 2Pac- 1994

- Common vs. Westside Connection- 1994

- Lil' Kim vs. Foxy Brown- 1997

- Cannibus vs. LL Cool J- 1997

- 50 Cent vs. Ja Rule- 2000

- Jay-Z vs. Nas- 2001

- Krs_One vs. Nelly- 2002

- Eminem vs. Benzino - 2002

- Nicki Minaj vs. Lil Kim- 2007

- Drake vs. Common- 2011

- Loaded Lux vs Calicoe – 2012 (Battle Rap)

Even though there could be some positive aspects, for audiences, to listen to artists beef, there are sometimes unfortunate aspects associated with beefs; specifically violence or death. Beefs and battle rap competitions can easily go from being a friendly competition over lyrical greatness to an all-out personal assault on someone's character, family, life, or lifestyle. There is *no* time out or hold back punches solution, during a beef or battle rap competition, especially since the 1990s, when beefs and battle rap competitions became popularized. In other words, beefs and battle rap competitions have gone from being an element of Hip Hop that is used to evoke artistic competition for entertainment purposes, to an all-out war that becomes personal. The Biggie and 2Pac beef displayed the highest level of negativity that beefs can cause within the Hip Hop culture. Biggie and Tupac's beef made entire coasts (east and west coasts) feud over which coast is more loyal to an artist; while the media instigated every aspect of dissension between the two rappers, who were once close friends. Unfortunately, Biggie and Tupac would both die and people would later realize that no one artist represented one area, because Hip Hop culture; specifically rap transcends boundaries; especially coastal.

Element 10

Collaborations- Collaborations are another fun aspect of Hip Hop culture, because collaborations allow artistic growth to be displayed. Collaborations allow two artists from different genres of music to collaborate and create new music or by remixing an already popularized song. Collaborations, also, provides an opportunity for artists who are up-and-coming to create music with an established artist or artists to gain artistic credibility and validity. Lastly, collaborations can expose artists to new or different fan bases, which can be financially lucrative. Collaborations, according to Hip Hop culture's history has two distinct dates of reference; 1981 and 1986. The 1981 collaboration includes Blondie featuring Fab Five Freddy in a song called, *Rapture.* The 1986 collaboration included Aerosmith and featured Run DMC in a song called, *Walk This Way.* Even though, Blondie's collaboration precedes the Aerosmith & Run DMC's collaboration, Hip Hop enthusiasts support the *Walk This Way* (1986), as the officially first rap collaboration, because the song featured rap artists rhyming, unlike Blondie's collaboration, which features her rapping, while Fab Five Freddie just appears in the video. Aerosmith & Run DMC's rock and rap collaboration helped create a sub-genre of Hip Hop called Rock Rap, which continues to bridge the gap between Rock-n-Roll and Hip Hop cultural roots.

Element 11

Fashion- Fashion is another important part of Hip Hop culture; especially concerning how trends are made and set within and outside of the culture. For example, one should not be surprised to learn that a majority of dj's, rap artists, breakdancers, and graffiti artists have developed and expanded profitable brands; specifically designed clothing, television shows, and electronics. Fashion trends were inspired by drug culture, initially. Designers like Dapper Dan made Gucci car seats, custom-made outfits, jumpsuits, velour sweatsuits and any other designer brands that people wanted. Fashion trends, such as jewelry, can dates as far back as African culture. Africa, was initially rich in resources; specifically diamonds, which ironically becomes a status symbol of success in Hip Hop culture; especially rappers. The array of bright colors and patterns associated with Hip Hop culture's fashion rose in the 1980s and continued to evolve into official brand name designer labels (once artists began to make more money commercially). Popularized designer labels included Tommy Hilfiger, Polo, Timberlands, First Downs, Goose downs,

Gazelles, Tom Fords, Bamboo Earrings, Throwback Jerseys, Hairstyles (Gumbies, Mushrooms, and Fades with designs). Eventually, Hip Hop entrepreneurs would begin to invest in their own clothing lines, such as F.U.B.U. (For.Us.By.Us by Daymond John), Phat Farm & Baby Phat (Russell Simmons) Sean Jean (Sean Combs), Roca-wear (Damon Dash, Jay-Z, and Kareem "Biggs" Burke), Wu-Gear (Wu-Tang Clan), Trukfit (Lil' Wayne's brand), OVO (Drakes Brand), as well as collaboration deals with Nike (Air Yeezy's/Kanye), Reebok (Rick Ross), Jordan Brand (OVO/Drake Jordans).

Element 12

Technology- Technological advances begin to influence Hip Hop culture in the early parts of the new millennium; specifically around the 2000s. With the consistent access to multiple social media platforms, up-and-coming artists; as well as established artists are allowed an innumerous amount of

exposure. Artists; especially up-and-coming or new artists are no

longer limited to being just a local celebrity, but can gain access

to people across the world without ever having met. Technology

has great benefits to Hip Hop culture, but can be detrimental to an

artist's craft. Some of the benefits include online collaborations

with artists in other states and countries and the ability to promote

ones music or talent beyond just the local radio station. Some

unfortunate aspects would be cultural misperceptions (people

believe the videos or lyrical content), piracy issues, and stealing

of intellectual property (lyrics, beats, or concepts stolen).

Element 13

Hustling (Legal & Illegal)- Hip Hop culture never has and

never will be exempt from hustling, because of the culture's

origins. Several record labels, rappers, dj's, graffiti artists, and breakdancers have succeeded because of legal and illegal

funding. Therefore, the best date attributed to this particular

element of Hip Hop would be forever. Hustling (legally and

illegally) has allowed Hip Hop culture to gain notoriety and

allowed those who are actively part of the culture instantaneously

rich; in many cases over-night.

Chapter 2

Crack Use to Be Wack, But Now, I'm in Love With The Co-Co, Molly, and Pills: Contradictions in Hip Hop

Hip Hop culture has evolved and matured, since the days when artists were just having fun and not all about the money, fame, and power. However, one thing that has become an unfortunate and reoccurring issue within the culture are the contradictions of the culture. From the boisterous and degrading hate-filled language concerning women to occasional and temporary references of adornment and love towards some women. Rhetorically speaking, how can a female determine her status in a world filled with contradictions about baby mama's, disloyal ho's, good girls, and wifey's? This is just one of the ongoing concerns and conflictions in Hip Hop; especially in regards to rap lyrics.

However, other pertinent concerns began to arise as Hip Hop was on the cusp of becoming recognizable beyond just street performances. The early 1970s marked a period where drug culture was promoted in songs like *Pusherman* (1972), from Curtis Mayfield. A snippet of Mayfields' *Pusherman* (1972):

I'm your Mama / I'm your Daddy/ I'm that nigga in the alley I'm your doctor / When in need/ Want some coke?/ Have some weed/ You know me I'm your friend/ Your main boy thick and thin/ I'm your Pusherman.../ Silent life of crime/ A man of odd circumstance/ A Victim of ghetto demands/ Feed me money for style/ And I'll let you trip for a while... / Ain't I clean/ Bad machine/ Super cool/ Super mean/ Dealin' good, for The Man/ Superfly, here I stand/ Secret stash, heavy bread/ Baddest bi***es in the bed

Unfortunately, by the time the 1980s arrived, people; especially African Americans, were no longer functional addicts, but full-blown crack addicts. The effects of crack left an indistinguishable mark on the psyche of the Hip Hop generation. The 1980s marked a devastating time in Hip Hop culture and would later become known as the crack era.

The impact of crack on the Hip Hop generation was deeper than just the addiction and devastation, but involved governmental hypocrisy. The very government and elected officials; specifically Ronald Wilson Reagan, would advise people to "Just Say No" and to seek counseling at local neighborhood rehabilitation centers. However, controversial reports and research would claim that the same government, who condemned and outlawed drugs and drug dealing, were *not* part of the solution, but instead part of the problem. Instead of writing an entire chapter about how Journalist Gary Webb suspiciously died, in 2004, from *two self-inflicted* gunshots to the head, after exposing the "Dark Alliance," in 1996. Or, choose to provide several concluding paragraphs about the CIA's involvement in the selling of narcotics by way of the Nicaraguan drug cartels, under the knowledge of President Reagan, I will instead focus on rap artists' controversial relationship with drugs. However, the focus of the discussion will be on the lyrical contradictions surrounding drugs, in Hip Hop. Hip Hop culture has an un-healthy relationship with drugs.

One would think that after seeing the devastation of how crack ripped through several communities, families, and friends, Hip Hop culture would never endorse, promote, glorify, or compliment any aspect of drug life or drugs. This sentiment would be difficult to uphold, because drugs have not just destroyed communities, but drugs have also made a lot of people money. Drugs have caused many deaths, but drugs have also inspired many rap records, fashion trends, and a false sense of manhood and strength. The unfortunate reality that surrounds the topic of drugs in Hip Hop; specifically rappers, is that rap lyrics fail to address the impact of drugs beyond the financial benefits, for a drug dealer. When rappers discuss drugs and drug culture as a lifestyle filled with money, fame, women, jewelry, cars, and alcohol, audiences (specifically those younger listeners who are impressionable) feel inclined to believe that they too can succeed in drug dealing. Even though drug dealing appears to have unlimited potential for success, many drug dealers end up dead, being shot, becoming a paraplegic, or in prison for multiple life sentences. The latter reality, prison, becomes a monumental staple in the permanent stagnation and limitation of one's ability to become successful and mature. Once a person is introduced to prison culture; especially young black and brown men, many scholars believe that cycle of prison becomes an inevitable and unchangeable cycle of dysfunction. The cycle of prison is heightened even more when a person's family and friends have been incarcerated. Prison culture develops and cultivates a prison mentality, which for scholars involves a cyclical process that includes a process of a person going to jail, coming from jail, or currently residing in jail (Dyson, 2007). This cycle becomes so engrained, in an individual, that some people begin to believe that prison is a "home" or a "rites of passage."

Drug culture; however, has also served as a double-edged sword in Hip Hop culture. Drug abuse and the selling of drugs have affected and incarcerated a lot of people's family members and friends, but the selling of drugs have also bought a lot of family and friends houses, cars, purses, clothing, furniture, jewelry, and sneakers (Foamposities (aka dope boy shoes) and Jordans). As haunting as these conflictions are; the results can appear to be just as beneficial as contradictory. Hip Hop culture is a culture that in 1986, made headline news, when a graffiti artist named Keith Haring painted a double-sided outdoor mural, on a New York City turnpike, proclaiming to the world, "Crack is Wack." The familiar phrase "Crack is Wack," was Hip Hop culture's attempt to declare how stupid one is to become addicted or affiliated with a drug that does nothing but devastate lives, families, and community. The same Hip Hop culture that declared, "Crack is Wack" now declares with adoration, "I'm in Love with the Co-Co," "Poppin' E-pills," and "Taking a bunch of Molly's."

How did Hip Hop culture; specifically rappers, go from demonizing the effects of crack, exposing the truth about governmental conspiracies surrounding drug dealing, and revealing the disproportionate sentencing rates between crack (which was considered a Black people's drug) and powdered cocaine (which was considered a White people's drug) to **now** declaring a love for a drug that has killed, permanently disabled, incarcerated, and destroyed families that can never be repaired? Has Hip Hop's popularity increased that much that the generations affected by this epidemic no longer exist or bear the marks of crack's grip on society; especially those growing up in Hip Hop? All of these questions are being raised, because these are questions that cause a potentially talent-filled movement to become hypocritical, just like the very movements that Hip Hop was created to challenge and change. How can Hip Hop be a voice for the voiceless, only out of convenience or guilt?

How can rap artist expose the truth of their experience without glorifying the parts that have and will lead people; especially young black and brown men into prison? When Miley Cyrus sings of popping Molly's, while twerking, and flying on a wrecking ball in her video, her song, videos, and artistry will be considered typical behavior from young woman experimenting with life. However, if Taneisha, from the inner city raps a song about taking pills and drinking, while doing a strip tease on a stripper poll, what will my artistry be considered? Is it wrong to bring race into the discussion? If so, why? Could it be that bringing race into the discussion reveals a level of hypocrisy, not just in Hip Hop, but society?

If Hip Hop culture; specifically rap lyrics are contradictory in language and behavior, one must look beyond the artist and discover who else demonstrates similar behavior. As childish as it may sound, some changes are only predicated on something else changing first. Things could always be better economically, socially, politically, and communally as it relates to better opportunities, income, housing, education, and overall community investment. However, being a victim of any systemic structure (racial, political, social, or economical) should never ignite one to go from being a victim to being a victimizer. Some of the children, who had drug addicted parents and family members, either ended up doing some form of drugs or avoided drugs all together; while other children eventually became drug dealers. Each scenario described, involving children, is relevant because whether the child engaged in illegal or illegal activities, surrounded drugs or avoided drugs all together, drugs had an undeniable effect on children, regardless. Rappers have gone from mocking crack and crack addicts (MC Shy-D song *Paula's on Crack*, in 1987), to explaining how to build your own crack enterprise (Notorious B.I.G.'s song *10 Crack Commandments*, in 1994), to explaining the struggles of those affected by the drugs (50 cent song, *A Baltimore Love Thing*, 2005), but then declaring an absolute love for the drug (O.T. Genasis song, *CoCo*, 2014). Maybe, rappers are only reflecting how a majority of society feels about drugs. For instance, if someone were to ask you, what is your stance on drugs, what would you say and would your answer be conflicting?

Chapter 3

Judge Not, Lest Ye Be Judged: Hip Hop's Sin

Older generations (specifically the Civil Rights generation) undeniably despise the vulgarity and language that is apparent in rap music. The degradation and forced submission of women to men for dominance, pleasure, and esteem is definitely a controversial topic within and outside of the culture. However, before anyone, including the older generations, begin to condemn Hip Hop culture; specifically the element of rap, one must also consider the historical issues, experiences, controversies, music, and people that existed before the Hip Hop generation began.

The Civil Rights Movement was comprised of male and female activists of all ethnicities; research suggests that women participating in the Civil Rights Movement outnumbered men. However, when looking back on the impact and icons of the Civil

Right Movement, most of the focus is primarily given to men. Women, although active in the Civil Rights Movement, are normally in the picture, but subservient and supportive to male leaders agendas. The roles of participants of men and women, during the Civil Rights Movement were reflective of the gender roles that have always plagued society. In other words, when it comes to fighting "isms", such as racism or classism, sexism is often the last issue to be solved; especially for an African American woman. Sexism has been in existence for a long time, in spite of women outnumbering men. Historical situations regarding gender roles, while fighting for equality, inspires one to ask the following philosophical question: Am I my race first or my gender?

This question can be easy or difficult to answer, depending on whom you speak too. In addition, to societal perceptions about gender roles and imagery another important, yet controversial person, begins to influence society, during the Civil Rights Movement. The "re-emergence" of the bootleg preacher had an unconscionable impact on gender roles and perceptions; especially in the church. For example, bootleg preachers typically wanted to control the congregants (mostly females) by using the Bible to control people, by using biblical scripture to justify or deny certain decisions. The bootleg preacher also wanted to collect tithes and offerings (money) from congregants (mostly female) and in some cases sexual favors from congregants (mostly female) for self-gain. Unfortunately, in many churches where the female congregants outnumber their male counterparts, women were used for various purposes, but rarely maintained notable positions in the church, because of patriarchal beliefs and domination (Dyson, 2007).

Another poignant person that emerged during the Civil Rights Movement was the Pimp. For example, Iceberg Slim

(Robert Beck), a renowned pimp, in Hip Hop culture, pimped women from all nationalities, wrote a number one best-selling book, and provided a foundation for a generation of men who would rather smack or disrespect a woman into being submissive to garner respect rather than show mutual respect. Iceberg Slim became the symbol and epitome of how pimping could be cool and a tool used to control women.

Iceberg Slim's (Robert Beck) charisma appears to be an evolved version of how women have and are constantly victimized, not just in rap music, but religiously as well. Without going through an entire theological explanation surrounding male and female relationships in the Bible, the best story to reference would be the story of Adam & Eve. The typical story of Adam and Eve (preached in most churches) revolves around disobedience and a piece of forbidden fruit (*Genesis 3:6-12*).

God (male) told Adam and Eve not to eat from the tree. One day, Eve and Adam walked passed the tree and Eve decided to grab the fruit and take a bite. After she took a bite, she then gave the fruit to Adam to eat. Immediately, both of them realized they were naked and hid. When God (male) visits the Garden of Eden, he begins to call out to Adam asking where he is. Adam ignores God (male) for a while and then speaks up, saying, I was hiding because I am naked. God (male) then asks Adam how do you know you are naked? Adam immediately replies, because the woman you gave me, Eve, gave me some fruit and I ate it. Then God (male) looks at Eve and says, "What have you done?"

This biblical story has been preached and taught for centuries and the loss of paradise was because of the disobedience of a woman, who Adam quickly blames, rather than protects. Just like Adam, Iceberg Slim unashamedly professed his thoughts and process of dominating a woman, especially when woman has been disobedient to his requests and demands. Iceberg Slim's mentality appears to be an evolved form of God & Adam, in the sense that pimps have the authority to curse (God cursed Eve) and blame (Adam blamed Eve) women. Iceberg Slim may appear to many people to be a despicable and deplorable person; however, Slim's profession of pimping was embraced and supported by many people; including other pimps, men, and in many instances women. Pimping would eventually become entertaining for some people, just like the Minstrel Show characters were, during the early 1800s. Iceberg Slim's pimp persona would become the inspiration for Black exploitation films and like *Shaft* (1971), *Superfly* (1972)), *The Mack* (1973), as well as the foundation for film characters such as Pretty Tony, Goldy, Huggy Bear. Pimping and being pimped was more alluring than being a so-called "Good Girl."

Many people may wonder what is the significance of bringing up gender roles and potential sexism, during the Civil Rights era, discussing the emergence of bootleg preachers, and referencing Iceberg Slim's pimp persona. For some people, the significance of these three references may be questionable; but for others these connections are relevant. The Civil Rights Movement was a Christian led movement, which means that principles in the Bible were a source for inspiration and motivation. The source of the Civil Rights Movement has also been a primary source for inspiration and motivation for bootleg preachers (in the past and currently). The same bootleg preachers who now have reality television shows and appear to promote money over whatever. Unfortunately, some of the same people who marched and protested, during the Civil Rights Movement alongside women, also had a possible disdain for women. Some of those men who attended church every Sunday had multiple affairs with other women. There is an old saying, "You cannot have your cake and eat it too." This statement was made to let people know that you cannot always have everything you want. Sometimes you are only given either-or choices, not both-and. Then one day, an unknown person; most likely a pimp, evolved the classic phrase, by adding the words, "Ain't that what you're supposed to do?" Implying that having cake and then eating the cake too is part of the full process of enjoying cake. In other words, the evolution of the original phrase to a newly evolved phrase suggests that having everything you want is still possible, if you think beyond what someone tells you. The bootleg preacher and pimps greatest gift is their ability to think and talk simultaneously beyond what someone else thinks, says, or believes.

Even though rap music speaks negatively about females, so do other important and essential figures in society and in our faith. An unescapable truth is formed early in our society and manifested in the gender roles that are created and within certain elements of one's faith that must be reconciled. The degradation of women, in rap songs and videos, are more than just a Hip Hop problem, but a societal problem. By no means does this excuse the behaviors or lyrical content of rap artists. However, as corny as the old cliché may sound; knowledge still is power. Until the previous generation teaches and explains truth rather than condemn and deny the current generations' ability to make mistakes, then change and growth will remain stagnant for both generations. In other words, if you never know what to change and why change is needed, then the cycle of dysfunction will continue and eventually be considered normal, rather than abnormal.

Chapter 4

Where Is The Love?: Rappers Relationship Statuses

When discussing whether love exists in Hip Hop, requires more than just a yes or no answer. To understand what love is in Hip Hop; specifically rap videos and rap lyrics, one must consider the bigger picture. Current rap songs and videos include two depictions of men and women. Men can be described as hyper-masculine and women as hyper-sexual. Hyper-masculinity is defined as exaggerated male stereotypical behavior, displayed in one's strength, aggression, and sexuality and is often directed towards women (Moshner and Sirkin, 1984).

Hyper-masculinity is manifested in typical rap lyrics and videos through profane discussions or depictions concerning drugs, violence, guns, alcohol, jewelry, travelling excursions, materialism, money, and domination of women through blatant and subtle sexual descriptions. The videos that the average rap video depicts all of these concepts and more. The over-saturation and a re-iteration of a man's dominance over women perpetuates sexism and degradation. Hyper-sexuality is defined as an oversexed obsession with the act of sex, which includes sexual activities and sexual fantasies (Rinehart and McCabe, 1997). Hyper-sexuality is manifested in typical rap lyrics and videos through profane discussions about sex, depictions of sexual activities, and sexual domination. For female rappers, hyper-sexuality is often revealed through the manipulation of men, materialism, money, travelling excursions, and profane discussions about sexual acts performed or received. The lyrical content and videos that female rappers currently create depicts an overstimulation of a woman's sexuality through constant sexual imagery. In other words, the motto, "sex sells," becomes

an essential part of a female rapper's appeal and success in Hip
Hop culture.

If Hip Hop culture is based on coming from nothing into
something, then rap lyrics paint the picture of those experiences
on route to becoming. A pivotal part of male rappers' experiences
involves personal relationships. The average rapper (male and
female) does not have a positive and functional representations of
male and female relationships; especially as it relates to
monogamy. The lack of positive personal relationships have an
interesting influence a rap artists' lyrical content; especially a male
rap artist. Because rap lyrics and videos rarely depict functional
relationships or conversations, many critics of rap music begin to
ask, "Where is the love, in Hip Hop?"

When discussing rap artists' perceptions and lyrical
content; Hip Hop enthusiast and critics alike would agree that love
and monogamy are virtually non-existent, in the rap element of

Hip Hop. Determining why rap artists do not feel compelled to discuss love and monogamy positively could be a relevant concern that is worthy of discussion. Understanding the current cultural, societal, and media views concerning love and relationships could explain and reinforce why rap artists' perceptions appear more negative than positive. For example, think about and answer the following questions, before proceeding to the next paragraph:

1. How would you describe Hip Hop culture's current view of love?
2. How would you describe the current societal view of love?
3. How would you describe Hip Hop culture's current perception about relationship statuses?
4. How would you describe current societal views about relationship statuses?

5. Can you recall and write down (*without having to research this information online*) at least <u>*five rap songs, including the artists*</u> that spoke positively about love and relationships?

As you look and consider your responses, think about how the cultural and societal perspectives are similar and different. Think about whether or not these perceptions are similar or different based on race, family structure (single or two-parent home), economic and political status, gender, or age. In other words, think about whether there are specific factors that influence how Hip Hop culture and current society perceives and promotes love and relationships.

Hip Hop culture originally included diversity lyrically; especially in regards to females, because females also have an investment in Hip Hop's culture, since its conception. In the first two-and-a-half decades of Hip Hop culture, rappers often included at least one song on their album that was positively dedicated to women. Think about it. Most of the rap albums created dating back from the 70s, 80s, and early-90s, included at least **one song** that reflected the love of a woman or the value of a relationship with a woman.

However, lyrical content, during the mid-90s shifted from typical topics like fun, partying, politics, life, friends, love, relationships, ceasing violence, and positivity to gangsta rap. The emergence of gangsta rap included more than just violence, guns, and drugs, but also included alternative perspectives about women. The lyrical content that begin to emerged in the mid-90s promoted hyper-masculinity and stereotypes about women that were similar to how a pimp treats, talks, and interacts with a ho. Lyrics such as "Lady in the Street/ But A Freak in the Bed," or "Take that Ho to the Ho-tel," as well as "Can't Turn A Ho Into A House Wife," and "I Got Hoes in Different Area Codes," becomes prevalent with each new rap song. Since the emergence of hyper-masculinity and hyper-sexuality, women are no longer adored, trusted, or respected, in rap music.

The alternative perspectives and depictions, of women, in rap lyrics and videos are reflective of the categorizations that females have been placed in; not just in Hip Hop culture, but society. If you think about the typical rap video, current reality television shows, current societal views, and various conversations with friends in person or on social media, women (specifically minority women and rap artists relationship statuses with women) are typically classified as either a: Baby Mama, New Age Ho, or a Good Girl/Wifey. Notice the graph depicting the typical male rapper's potential relationship statuses and experiences with these three women while attempting to become a successful rapper.

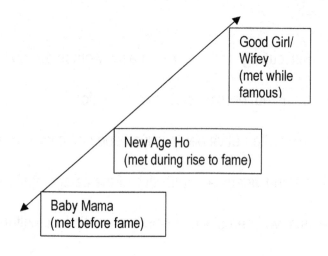

When discussing the roles of women, in an average rap artist's life, the relationship status can be filled with complexities. The typical male rap artist starts his career at the bottom of the chart (most likely broke) and becomes more famous, eventually being able to make a living from rapping. However, with success comes various relationships that can make being successful extremely stressful.

The first tier of the relationship chart starts at the bottom (specifically bottom left). At this point, the rappers career is non-existent and he most likely has a Baby Mama. The Baby Mama is typically a young female that went to middle or high school with the rap artist and the two dated or had sex (out of wedlock), which led to a baby or babies being born. The Baby Mama could be the mother of between one and five of the rappers' children. Typically, at this stage (the first tier), if the rapper and her decide to remain in a relationship, the Baby Mama serves as an important person in the up-and-coming rappers' life. The Baby Mama may also provide money (if the rapper is not stealing drugs), for the rapper's clothing, recording studio sessions, or travelling expenses. The Baby Mama also takes care of the children; especially on those late nights when the rapper is at the studio recording music. The Baby Mama is also important to the esteem of the rapper because she appears to love him unconditionally. In other words, she sees his potential and is able to love him even though he is broke. The rapper appreciates these attributes, in spite of the occasional arguments surrounding finances, bills, and questions about when his career will evolve from just a hobby to a career.

The second tier of the relationship chart represents growth and newfound exposure in the rappers career. At this stage, the rapper is gaining a local following and becoming what some would call a "Hood Star" or "Hood Famous." At this point of his career, the rapper is performing at local nightclubs, the local radio station is playing his songs, and people are beginning to recognize the rapper at various venues or events. The rapper is working more than ever and beginning to see some level of success in his career. The rapper has to spend most of his days in the studios, constantly using some form of social media platforms to communicate with fans (rappers in the 1980s and 1990s relied heavily on radio stations and word-of-mouth), and spends more time away from home to perform or attend parties. All of these activities are a requirement for the rap artist to gain success, remain relevant, and build a strong fan base; especially when his album premieres. Most of the rappers' performances are at clubs late at night; making it difficult for the Baby Mama to attend. Because the Baby Mama is taking care of the children at home and most likely has to take care of the children (as if she is a single-parent), a disconnect begins to occur between the rapper and his Baby Mama.

Even though the rapper understands how much his Baby Mama is doing, the rapper still wishes and wants her to be at his performances to support him. The Baby Mama's inability to meet his demands causes the rapper to develop a vulnerability. As the rapper is gaining local status, he is getting more attention and the ho's at the club are screaming and dancing every time that he performs. However, at every show, the rapper notices one particular female (New Age Ho) that seems to attend every one of his performances. What makes this particular female (New Age

Ho) intriguing to the rapper is her appearance, her confidence, and her love for his music. The "New Age Ho" does not only dance to rappers music, while in the club, but she is raps every word to his songs, as if she wrote the lyrics herself.

The rapper desires to remain faithful to his Baby Mama, but with each performance where she is not present, makes it easier for the woman who is present. The sexual chemistry continues to build, between the rapper and this woman (New Age Ho), from afar through admiration. Eventually, the rapper cheats and has sex with this woman (New Age Ho) and things become even more complex. The sexual chemistry and encounter with the "New Age Ho," is amazing to the rapper. The rapper feels slightly guilty for being unfaithful to his Baby Mama; however, he does not feel complete remorse because he feels comfortable and supported by the woman (New Age Ho). After having sex with the woman (New Age Ho); instead of going to sleep after sex, the rapper talks with the woman (New Age Ho) about everything ranging from his drama with his Baby Mama to his aspirations, and even his personal interests, like sports, friends, and hobbies. Eventually, the rapper begins to spend more time with the woman (New Age Ho) and less time with his Baby Mama. As the Baby Mama expresses the need for affection, attention, and communication from the rapper, the rapper directs his affection, attention, and communication towards the other woman (New Age Ho). The rapper, even though he is only "Hood Famous" begins to buy gifts or provide money to the woman (New Age Ho).

The moment that the rapper begins to show the woman (New Age Ho) more attention than his Baby Mama, is the moment that the woman (New Age Ho) is no longer interested or attracted to the rapper. What makes this woman a "New Age Ho" is her lack of interest in anything, but self-gain. The New Age Ho, are different from women who just sleep with a rapper for bragging purposes, a purse, some shoes, or to eventually fall in love. The "New Age Ho" is not playing the game for love or even keeps, but for opportunities. The "New Age Ho" realizes that the quickest way to a man's wallet is through his ego. The "New Age Ho" builds the rappers esteem, overly compliments the rapper, all while gaining access to his money and inner circles, which sometimes includes access to other potentially rich and wealthy men.

A "New Age Ho" is no longer dependent on a pimp or a man, to tell her what to think, but actually will disagree with the rapper without hesitation (publically or privately). In other words, the "New Age Ho" is confident enough to know that speaking her mind is not something that will decrease the rapper's interest in her. The "New Age Ho" is confident, self-determined, and methodical in her approach. The "New Age Ho" has more than just a G.E.D. and may have attended college (2-year or 4-year) or currently attends college. The "New Age Ho" is self-motivated and typically does not have children; however, if she does, she only has one child. Most likely, someone else takes care of that one child (a family member; the child's father, or her mother) on a full-time basis, so that the "New Age Ho" is able to pursue what she perceives as success. The goal of this "New Age Ho" is to play the game to win and win more than just a few times.

The third tier of the relationship chart, as it pertains to the rapper, is the Good Girl/ Wifey. The "Good Girl/Wifey" status is the last tier of the chart and symbolizes the rapper at the height of his success. At this stage, the rapper has realized that the "New Age Ho" is not interested in playing house or becoming wifey; therefore, the rapper moves on to date or marry a woman that he believes fits his current lifestyle. By this point, the rapper and the Baby Mama are not speaking to one another and have not seen each other in months, maybe even years. The "Good Girl/Wifey"

is unique and most likely different from all of the other women that

the rapper has met, had sex with, or dated. "The Good

Girl/Wifey" is appealing to the rapper, because she is self-

sufficient, goal driven, and typically does not have any children; if

she does, she only has one child. The "Good Girl/Wifey" has at

least one college degree, if not more, and appears to love and

admire the man that the rapper has become, without ever

knowing the details of the rappers past. The rapper and the

"Good Girl/Wifey," eventually, move into a home together, gets

engaged or married; making the "Wifey" status either a potential

or official name. Unfortunately, as wonderful as the "Good

Girl/Wifey" appears to be, the sexual chemistry that he had with

the "New Age Ho" is missing. As a result, the rapper most likely

finds himself cheating with the "New Age Ho" knowing that she

does not want, need, or desire a relationship with the rapper. The rapper continues to give the "New Age Ho" money and gifts, in spite of the reality of their relationship status, which is based on occasional sex, money, and conversations that the rapper cannot have with his Baby Mama or the Good Girl/Wifey.

With the rappers new found success, home, and "Good Girl/Wifey" comes another responsibility. The rapper must rebuild his relationship with his children; the children he had with his Baby Mama. The children come and visit the rappers new big house, sees the new cars, goes shopping, and realizes how much better life is at daddy's house. The children then go back home and begin to tell the Baby Mama everything that they saw and experienced, while with daddy and the "Good Girl/Wifey."

At this point, the "Baby Mama" has had enough of the rappers' promises, the occasional I love you's, and meaningless sex. The easiest and best way for the Baby Mama to regain a sense of power would be to go to the courthouse and file for child support. Throughout the rapper's climb towards success, the Baby Mama most likely believed in the possibility of marriage and a happily ever life with the rapper. However, the fact that the rapper has a seemingly fairytale life with a "Good Girl/Wifey" is not only insulting, but offensive to the Baby Mama, who had remain loyal before the fame. Once child support is filed, the judge sets a date for the child support hearing and most of the time the judge rules in favor of the Baby Mama. The child support ruling often mandates the rapper pay an enormous amount of money, ranging from a minimum of 5,000.00 a month to 50,000.00 a month. The typical rapper normally appeals the child support amount and requests a decrease in the amount, because the required payment exceeds the rapper's income. Even though the Baby Mama thinks that rapper is lying about his finances to avoid making payments, he is most likely telling the truth.

The reality is that most rappers do not own most of the property or cars. The home is rented and the car is leased. All the cash money has most likely been spent on entourages, parties, jewelry, vacations, strip clubs, alcohol, drugs, clothes, shoes, flights, lavish restaurants, and occasional gifts for random females, or the "Good Girl/Wifey." Additional money (specifically the unaccounted for amounts of cash) has been given to the "New Age Ho." Therefore, when rappers appear on television looking like a billionaire, the rapper is most likely just a stressed out thousand-aire. The ideal life of a rapper can appear more stressful with money, then the life of the rapper before the money.

After reviewing the chart and reading the explanation for the typical relationships surrounding the average rapper, the explanation may cause some men and male rappers to disagree with the idea of a woman or any woman having that kind of power or control; especially a "New Age Ho." The categorizations may also some controversy or some women to question their position

or status on this chart. However, please keep in mind that these

categorizations are not based on how a woman may view herself

or her position (personally), but based on how a male (specifically

a male rapper) perceives women, in Hip Hop culture. The various

rap song lyrics make constant references about these three

categorizations of women. In spite of the potential offense or

perceptions, no one woman could or should want to ascribed to fit

any of these three categories, described in this chart, because

each woman struggles with establishing a functional and secure

relationship with such a complicated person; the male rapper.

Like everything in life there are some exemptions to the rule;

however, when considering those rappers who you believe are

exemptions, to these categorizations, please delve closely into

whether or not that relationship (that is being considered) has been an open relationship, a break-up period in the relationship, a monogamous relationship, or a polygamous relationship.

Although these adaptations could be used strictly as a standard for relationship statuses, in Hip Hop culture, one may find these descriptions present in society. When various media platforms begin to promote the portrayal of women as Thot's, Ho's, Baby Swallowers, Bi**hes, and all types of other words, as if this is the norm, then rap lyrics should be the least of one's worries. Is the apparent silence a sign of acceptance or have we progressed enough, as women, to know not to answer to anything less than your birth name these days? Has society become immune to offensive lyrics made towards women in music? Is this why when a rap artists says, when I call her a "Bi**h," I am not talking about you. I am talking about her. To which the female fan replies, "O, Ok." Or, is this why women appear to embrace negativity and make negative comments about women by saying,

"I ain't no Bi**h or Ho," but then simultaneously declare

themselves as Boss Bi**hes or Bad Bi**hes?" The enjoyment and

detachment while listening to music is complex; especially when

the song includes a nice beat. When listening, endorsing, or

enjoying music, the choice still belongs to the individual, not the

one who criticizes those who choose to listen to offensive or

vulgar rap songs.

Music was created with a purpose, which by many

accounts includes the freedom of expression. However,

everything should be done so in balance. One should be able to

find just as many complimentary love songs in Hip Hop as one

finds offenses. Lauryn Hill back in 1998, in her hit song,

Superstar,

> Yo hip-hop, started out in the heart
> Now everybody tryin' to chart
> I thought our art was supposed to inspire
> Music is supposed to take us higher

Now tell me your philosophy

On exactly what an artist should be

Should they be someone with prosperity

And no concept of reality?

What happened to being secure in not being the typical, average,

or the norm? What happened to expressing yourself, without

offending others? What happened to the checks and balance

system of respect based on constructive criticism? What

happened to wrong is wrong? What happened to two-way

listening and introspection, after a disagreement? Instead,

nobody wants to listen, but everybody wants to talk. If Hip Hop

culture needs to be drastically changed, so does society, because

Hip Hop is a reflection of society, whether or not one agrees or

chooses to redirect the blame.

Chapter 5

Bridging the Gap: Why Can't We All (Older and Younger Generations) Just Get Along?

Hip Hop is a culture that is founded on the idea of turning nothing into something. In other words, Hip Hop culture derives from a level of self-sufficiency. The elements of Hip Hop culture emerged from the creativity of Dj's like Kool Herc and includes business pioneers like Russell Simmons & Rick Rubin (Def Jam), Chris Lighty (Violator), J. Prince (Rap-A-Lot), and Sean Combs (Bad Boy), and game changers like Sean Carter (Jay-Z), Kimberly Jones (Lil' Kim), Onika Tanya Maraj (Nicki Minaj), Kanye West (Yeezy), William Griffin Jr. (Rakim), Tupac Shakur (2Pac), Brad Jordan (Scarface), Marshall Mathers (Eminem), and Curtis Jackson (50 Cent) who are self-taught leaders and innovators, in the Hip Hop Culture. When people look at the larger impact of

Hip Hop as a culture and not just a genre of music, defined by rap lyrics, the culture appears to be a great opportunity for people (specifically young African American males) to accrue a level of influence and affluence beyond athletics. However, since Hip Hop's conception; specifically since the 1990s gangster rap emergence, major criticism has followed and defined the culture negatively.

Many outspoken Civil Rights' leaders and Hip Hop cultural critics like Al Sharpton, Jesse Jackson, Delores Tucker, and Stanley Crouch believe that Hip Hop culture's local and globally impact has been more negative than positive. Critic Stanley Crouch has on more than a few occasions called current Hip Hop culture; specifically the rappers, modern day Minstrel Show performers. Critics also believe that the constant negative categorizations of women, derogatory depictions of women in the video, the use of the "N" word, and the promotion of guns and violence have overshadowed any signs of hope in the culture. Rap music is not perfect and constantly reflects immaturity and inconsistency. However, rap music has and continues to struggle with remaining authentic and reflective of the human experiences; which includes the good and the bad.

Unfortunately, when a discussion ensues between these two groups (those belonging to the Civil Rights Generations and the Hip Hop Generations), the conversation shifts to blame rather than empowerment and betterment. In addition, critics often classify all rappers as the same, in regards to talent, influence, affluence, and lyrical content. Many unknowledgeable critics believe that there is no differentiation between a Common, a Soulja Boy, 2Chainz, or a Kendrick Lamar lyrically or from an artist maturation process. The inability to realize the diversity of artistry, lyrical content, and elements of Hip Hop culture creates a tension where those belonging to Hip Hop culture; specifically rap artists, are always on the defensive and critics are always accusatory. As criticism of Hip Hop Culture continues, hypocrisy begins to emerge because those belonging to an older generation appear to present their experiences as flawless and faultless. In other words, maturity often comes with age, failures (not just success), and learned experiences. Those belonging to the older generations were once young, immature, criticized by previous generations, and imperfect; yet the criticism appears to be hypocritical, rather than constructive.

The expectation and mandate for every artist to be mature personally, lyrically, and artistically is a difficult request, because each artist differs in age, life experience, wisdom, and thought-processes. Hip Hop is one of the leading genres of music that did not emerge from the church or was initially embraced by the church. Hip Hop's roots were formed in the streets and the streets do not care about morals and principles, only survival.

The expectations placed on Hip Hop culture cannot be examined with the same standard or expectations of previous genres of music or previous generations. In other words, those who created and helped cultivate Hip Hop culture experience(d) the worse sides of life, which includes experiences based on:

lack of support from older generations, deaths of loved ones, imprisonment, criticism, being doubted by family members and strangers, witnessing murder, dying young, criminality, being products of broken homes, having children while still a child, drug addictions, being victims of rape, abuse, being hated, frustration, fear, failure, depression, being bullied, embarrassment, being raised in poverty, experiencing injustice (educationally, politically, socially, economically, and environmentally).

The inability, for older generations and critics of Hip Hop, to identify the struggles from which Hip Hop artists emerge, creates further tension and division between these two generations.

Being able to offer *constructive* criticism, while still complementing and commending the positive aspects of the Hip Hop culture is essential. The Civil Rights and Hip Hop generation has more in common than realized and are co-dependents in one another's growth. For example, those who are part of the Civil Rights generation had to fight for everything and everyone; even when their voices, opinions, concerns, and needs were threatened. The same can be said about those individual's belonging to the Hip Hop generation. The ability to express one's self uncensored was learned and taught from the Civil Rights generation.

Unfortunately, when the Hip Hop generation is compared to the Civil Rights generation, many people feel as if the comparison is blasphemous and inaccurate. The Civil Rights generation was a voice for the voiceless, just as the Hip Hop generation has been for its followers. The Civil Rights generation has been racially profiled, murdered, image conscious, gang affiliated, and arrested for simply trying to fulfill "The American Dream," just as the Hip Hop generation has been. In spite of all the negative, immature, and current issues surrounding the Civil Rights generation, the Civil Rights Movements legacy has not been deemed ineffective or irrelevant; therefore, why do many Civil Rights leaders and critics pre-maturely diminish and inaccurately predict the impact of the Hip Hop generation's role in society?

In 2012, a disagreement between Harry Belafonte and Jay-Z occurred that reflected the dissension between these two generations. Harry Belafonte (86 years old at time of interview) who is a well-known actor (*Carmen Jones, 1954 and Calypso, 1956*), singer [specifically songs like *Day-O*, 1956], political leader in the Civil Rights Movement, personal and close friend of Dr. King, and current advocate for equality, has spent his entire life giving to others, fighting for equality, and against injustices. On

would think that Harry Belafonte would extend grace and reach

out, privately first, to teach those who he deems unaware, before

making any public assertions.

In spite of Harry Belafonte's personal experiences, on

August 8, 2012, Belafonte's interview with *The Hollywood*

Reporter, was published. In the interview, Belafonte was asked,

"Are you happy with the image of members of minorities in

Hollywood today?" Belafonte (2012), response was:

> *Not at all. They have not told the history of our people, nothing*
> *of who we are. We are still looking. We are not determinated.*
> *We are not driven by some technology that says you can kill*
> *Afghans, the Iraqis or the Spanish. It is all -- excuse my*
> *French – s**t. It is sad. And I think one of the great abuses of*
> *this modern time is that we should have had such high-profile*
> *artists and powerful celebrities. But they have turned their*
> *backs on social responsibility. That goes for Jay-Z and*
> *Beyoncé, for example. Give me Bruce Springsteen, and now*
> *you're talking. I really think he is black...Belafonte also*

asserts, one white star could teach black luminaries a thing or two about social awareness.

Harry Belafonte's response is understandable; especially given his lifetime fight for social, political, economic, educational, and environmental equality, as well as his fight against injustice. However, Hip Hop enthusiasts would consider Belafonte's response harsh and unfortunate. Belafonte's and other Civil Rights leaders' critique of the Hip Hop generation's lack of significance and relevance based solely on financial affluence and social popularity. In other words, if you have money and popularity, then you are required to create social, political, and economic change. The notion of using your influence to create change is not the problem. The problem is when you create a forcible and automatic mandate on every person who has money and social popularity. Making one person or entire culture responsible for change is problematic and creates more resistance than support; especially in Hip Hop culture. No one person, group of people, or a sole culture should be responsible. Instead, everyone should work together and cultivate support from each culture's group of influential leaders. Belafonte and other critics of Hip Hop culture have failed to understand that the Hip Hop generation grew up in a different era, where politics and governmental change is viewed with suspicion not confidence. Belafonte and other critics of Hip Hop culture also have failed to realize that Hip Hop culture is mostly comprised of people who grew up "fatherless," which means that those who are part of the Civil Rights generation are also part of the group that left those born in the 1970s (like Jay-Z) fatherless.

Belafonte's response and critique of Jay-Z and Beyoncé is similar to the criticism that W.E.B. DuBois received for attempting to promote the Talented 10th concept. For Belafonte and any other Civil Rights leaders to say that Jay-Z has turned his back on social responsibility is a harsh critique that is unsubstantiated. In other words, Jay-Z, may not meet the standard set by Belafonte or other Civil Rights leaders by publicizing his political or social actions; however, Jay-Z's impact should not be considered any less valuable than his predecessors' impacts. Jay-Z has funded scholarships, given back to his community locally and globally, re-invested in areas that needed de-gentrification, as well as contributed to global needs of communities by building wells and funding educational needs, in Africa.

There are too many instances when the Hip Hop culture has to battle outside critics, while simultaneously battling their elders (older generations). Fighting against outside people is different than fighting from with people who are your family (direct descendants culturally). Belafonte's response not only exposes the unfortunate dissension between two groups, but also exposes the lack of mentorship. An old adage says, "It is not what you say, but how you say it." Belafonte's approach and critique of

Jay-Z's and Beyoncé's lack of social responsibility could have

been articulated differently. Belafonte's critique of Jay-Z and his

wife Beyoncé's impact automatically creates a level of hostility

from Jay-Z. Because Belafonte's comments were made public,

before a private consultation with the Carter's, Jay-Z was already

on the defense. Before reporters asked Jay-Z about his thoughts,

a rap verse was already being recorded. Jay-Z chose to respond,

just as any rap artist would, when called out publically by another

artist, by creating a song; called *Nickels and Dimes*, on his 2013

Magna Carta album. Jay-Z's lyrical response was:

> *I'm just trying to find common ground/ 'Fore Mr. Belafonte*
> *come and chop a nigga down/ Mr. Day O, major faaaaa--il/*
> *Respect these youngins' boy, it's my time now/ Hublot*
> *homie..two door homie/ You don't know all the s**t I do for*
> *the homies./... Oh, I'm clear as water/ And just for clarity,*
> *my presence is charity/ My flow is a gift, philanthropist/*
> *Everybody around me rich, or will be/ Baby boy I promise*

you this, or kill me/ And when a nigga go as the old adage go/ You die rich or you die a disgrace/ So just let me grow/ Y'all don't deserve me/ My flow unearthly/ The greatest form of giving is anonymous to anonymous/ So here y'all go, I promise this.

Was Jay-Z's lyrical response too harsh for Harry Belafonte's statement? Was Jay-Z's response inappropriate and disrespectful to his elder, Harry Belafonte's age, career accomplishments, and social impact? Should an older person have to give respect to get respect? These three questions and more are essential to determining why these two generations appear to have such disdain and resentment; considering how important each group is to one another's future. Whether you agree or disagree with Harry Belafonte or Jay-Z, the discussion of who is right is overshadowed by decades of constant criticism and not enough support or encouragement. Growth is not just a one-sided attribute; especially when trying to evoke sustainable change.

Chapter 6

Self-Made or Man Made: The Ladies of Rap, But Only Room for One Queen

When discussing women in Hip Hop culture; specifically the female rapper, several topics and concerns could be mentioned. However, from an historical perspective, women in Hip Hop; specifically rap will always include topics of controversy. Most of today's female rap videos depict the same controversial images that males are reprimanded for having, by rap critics, civil rights leaders, and feminist. Female rap videos also reveals an over-stimulation and re-iteration a woman's sexuality through constant sexual imagery. In other words, the motto, "sex sells," is still an essential part of rap music and videos. The only difference now is that a female rapper's sex appeal can breed success in the culture.

Before discussing the names of various female rap

pioneers and what constitutes success for a female rapper, the

obvious must be stated:

> Current rap culture does not appear to embrace females in
> the same way that male rappers are accepted. Also,
> female rappers who have been able to dominate the rap
> industry often have done so with limited lyrical content
> (mostly about sex, sexual positions, and clothing brands)
> with the least amount of clothing as possible.

Now, that the basic argument concerning female rappers has

been made, discussing the reasons why female rappers have a

tough time acquiring long-term sustainable success in Hip Hop

culture becomes essential. Like many historical movements in

society and popular culture, males tend to be in the forefront,

even though women typically maintain a presence or leadership

position within the movement. In spite of women, being present

at the start of Hip Hop culture and having such a monumental role in the musically inspired movement, women have always struggled to be respected, admired, and perceived as equal or greater than their male counterparts.

In other words, the most non-talented male rapper may receive more influence, affluence, and radio play than the best female lyricist in Hip Hop. The most dominating factors that contribute to this level of inequality include gender, sex appeal, and lyrical content. In other words, consider the Soulja Boy phenomenon that occurred in 2007. Soulja Boy took Hip Hop culture by storm with songs that included nonsensical lyrics, a catchy hook, nice beats, and a dance. His total sales and relevancy is still greater than the average female rapper, in Hip Hop. Unfortunately, a woman needs more than lyrics, a catchy hook, nice beats, and a dance to become a mediocre female rapper. Now, think about this and ask yourself the following question: Any female that has had any kind of rap success, including the rise to power to become the "Queen of Rap" has done so by:

A) Herself (self-made)
B) A Man (man-made)
C) Herself (self-made) and A Man (man-made)

As you think about the answer, make sure you choose wisely and consider the history of the female rapper and females throughout history. Even though women outnumber men, men control and have controlled society consistently. In the words of James Brown, *This Is a Man's World* (1966) and Hip Hop culture; specifically rap culture is no exception to this rule. There appears to be a direct correlation between a female rapper's success in Hip Hop and the male rapper who mentors her. In other words, if a female rapper desires success, in Hip Hop, she must link up with a successful male rapper who can validate her rapping skills

93

and cultivate her commercial appeal. What is even more important to understand is that the female rapper who gains success appears to be forever indebted to that particular male rapper, because without that male rapper, her career will be short lived. Examples of the connections between female rappers and their male counterparts are present in the following careers:

- Salt and Pepa & Hurby Azor
- Mc Lyte & Milk D & Dj Giz
- Queen Latifah & Dj King Gemini and Fab 5 Freddy
- Lil Kim & The Notorious B.I.G.
- Yo-Yo & Ice Cube
- Missy Elliot & Timbaland
- Trina & Trick Daddy
- Nicki Minaj & Lil Wayne
- Iggy Azalea & T.I.

As progressive as American society has become, the fact that females appear to need a male rappers' influence to become successful, could explain why there is a willing participation by female rappers to appear oversexed lyrically and physically. In other words, sex has and continues to sell; especially in the entertainment industry, so why would anyone deviate from what sells? The reality that sex is commercially appealing has continually plagued Hip Hop culture; specifically rap music. Each generation, especially female artists, have dealt with the conflictions surrounding whether or not to embrace the notion of being a sex symbol. Some woman chose to embrace the notion and flip the script as opposed to fight against the industry's standard mantra for success. In other words, rather than be sexualized or dominated by a man, some women chose to dominate men, by using sex as a form of power. Take a moment and conduct research on the following women:

1. Bessie Smith (*I'm Wild About A Thing, 1929*)
2. Pam Grier (*Foxy Brown, 1974*)
3. Millie Jackson (*F**K You Symphony, 1982*)

Each woman signified the level and progress of women and self-dominance regarding their sexuality as a means for empowerment, not degradation. The confliction between being disrespected and empowering one's self with the same disrespectful words seems hypocritical to some male and female listeners. The disrespect of women, in Hip Hop culture, is heightened and questioned further, when women direct that same level of disrespect towards other women.

When discussing female rappers in Hip Hop culture; one has to go beyond the relationship between males and females, but the antagonistic relationship between female rappers and other female rappers. There appears to be a notion that only one "Queen of Rap" can exist within Hip Hop culture. The fact that women cannot support one another or present a united front within Hip Hop culture is unfortunate. To make matters worse, the number of successful female rappers, in Hip Hop, has declined drastically, since the 1990s. Part of the decline may be due to racism, sexism, or simply because females would rather hate one another than elevate one another. For example, the recent 2014 *XXL Magazine's* choice of Iggy Azalea, as the first female rapper ever to appear on the cover of the rap magazine, created controversy within the Hip Hop community. Questions surrounding the *XXL's Magazine's* decision range from:

1. Why did it take so long for a female to grace the cover?
2. Why is the first female to grace the cover of the magazine white?
3. If Iggy Azalea is the first to grace the cover, what does that say about the other female rappers (like Da Brat, Sole', Yo-Yo, Left-Eye, Queen Latifah, Trina, Lauryn Hill, Rah Digga, Missy Elliot, Mia X, Eve, Charlie Baltimore, Foxxy Brown, Amil, Queen Pen, Lil' Kim, Nicki Minaj, and others) that preceded her?

4. Why was a female rapper from outside of the United States chosen to grace the cover?

5. Lastly, why was a female rapper whose lyrics on song, entitled, 2011 song D.R.U.G.S (which is an acronym for Directing. Reality. Undermining Governed. Systems), appeared to reveal racially sensitive references to being a runaway slave allowed to grace the cover of the magazine? The lyrics to the song were: Tire marks, tire marks / Finish line with the fire marks / When the relay starts, I'm a runaway slave-master/ Shi**n' on the past, gotta spit it like a pastor.

After asking these questions, one must wonder if these concerns are relevant or irrelevant. *XXL Magazine* started in 1997, and the birth of *XXL Magazine* coincided with an important time in Hip Hop history; especially for the female rapper. According to *BE Magazine* (2001), the 1990s was a monumental period in Hip Hop for the female rapper because this decade "saw more female rappers emerge (specifically 24) than both the 80s and the 2000s combined." No matter what your opinion is on this particular topic concerning the impact of female rappers on Hip Hop culture, one cannot ignore the connection between Iggy Azalea's rise to success in Hip Hop and the connection to the historic issues that have plagued the African American community; specifically African Americans in entertainment.

Maybe, Iggy Azalea's status would not be questioned, if female rappers were unified, in their stance as females and not focused on just being the top female. Maybe, one day, Nicki, Iggy, and Lil' Kim could create a song together, like Lil' Kim did in 1997, with *Ladies Night (Not Tonight Remix)*, to show unification among females and not separation. How can a female claim to be a Queen of Rap, when the system is rigged with a false sense of domination? The Queens' success is contingent on the King's success. There is no transference of power or true sense of power; because the definition of Queen is independence not dependence. Instead, of arguing over who is the Queen of Rap,

maybe female rappers should be building an empire of Queens

that represent Hip Hop, in all facets, through collaborations, and

mentorships. There is room enough for every female rapper, in

Hip Hop, but the ongoing nonsensical arguments and social

media rants only leads to the destruction of the culture for all

females.

Chapter 7

Maintaining Authenticity in Hip Hop

If a rapper said it, then it must be true,...right? Discussions about authenticity in Hip Hop culture; specifically rap artists and lyrics, has always been a point of contention. Part of the reason for such contention surrounds Hip Hop's initial promotion of the culture being the raw and uncut side of street life for teenagers growing up on the cusp (1970s generation) and during the crack epidemic (1980s generation). Hip Hop culture, like most (if not all music genres) sought to tell a story that was similar to previous genres of music, but more intentional, blatant, and perverse. In other words, the Hip Hop generation refused to speak in coded messages, use obscure metaphors, or be censored.

Hip Hop culture's ability to remain true to the essence of the crafts described in the initial elements of Hip Hop (graffiti, dj'ing, breakdancing, and mc'ing) made the culture and the audiences believe in the authenticity of the movement. Authenticity is an important conversation, when discussing Hip Hop culture; especially current day rappers. Conversing about the authenticity of a rap artist, these days, is like discussing one's religious beliefs. What makes you believe in a rapper's status as the best and where is your proof for such a declarative statement? In spite of one's declaration, most people end up rejecting one's notion of which rappers keep it real versus those who are inauthentic, while others sub-consciously consider the argument, and others suggest another rapper to consider.

One foundational aspect surrounding authenticity is transparency. How transparent has the rap artist, been about his or her life experiences before and after fame? Some casual hearers, fans, critics, and Hip Hop enthusiasts of Hip Hop have varied reasons for caring or not caring about an artists' authenticity. However, if Hip Hop culture is predicated on being a "voice for the voiceless," "speaking truth to power," and being "real," then what has inspired the current and apparent proverbial shift in thinking? What made most people fall in love with Hip Hop culture was the "truth" in Hip Hop. The "truth" is never easy to handle and even harder to understand, given the complexities.

Therefore, when a rap artist painted a picture of a life's harsh reality, which included violence, drugs, parties, sex, pimping, alcohol, and several other activities, listeners absorbed every word. Rappers, initially, painted pictures that were not just abstract, but pictures that were similar (if not the same) as the lives experienced by the listener. Rappers told the stories for those who could not or did not have time to tell their own story. Rappers rhymed with conviction and dedication. Unfortunately, the love that was initially felt, when Hip Hop started, is now questionable and has many wondering whether inauthenticity has depreciated Hip Hop culture; specifically the art of rapping.

Further discussions about the authenticity of rappers have often hinged on two modern day classifications: underground or commercial. Supposedly, these two categorizations provide insight about who contributes to the decline of authenticity in rap. For example, the assertion of supporters of underground rap suggest that rappers who have become commercial have chosen money over artistry, beats over lyrics, and fame over loyalty. While those supporters of commercial rappers who chose to remain underground have chosen poverty over stability, lyrics over influence, and stagnation over adaptation. These two distinctions between underground and commercial rappers, although differing, have credence to the discussion of authenticity.

However, the discussion does not cease with just these two categorizations of rappers.

Most rappers (if not all) who have achieved great success (affluence and influence) in Hip Hop culture; especially rappers, were once underground rappers. In other words, "those people over there" use to be "the people right here." Every genuine rap artist desires to escape from the dungeons of obscurity to platforms of recognition. Rap artists, specifically commercially successful rap artists, are constantly sharing personal accounts of their struggles in spite of fame and money. Notorious B.I.G.'s words, "Mo Money, More Problems," were inexplicably truthful; especially to those who believe that money actually solves problems. Here are a few rap verses from artists like Eminem, Nicki Minaj, and J. Cole lyrics, who reveal the complexities that come with success (commercial appeal): Eminem in the song, *The Way I am (2008)* states:

I'm so sick and tired of being admired/ That I wish that I would just die or get fired/ And dropped from my label, let's stop with the fables/ I'm not gonna be able to top on "My Name Is"/ And pigeon-holed into some poppy sensation/ To cop me rotation at rock-n-roll stations/ And I just do not got the patience/ To deal with these cocky Caucasians who think/ I'm some wigger who just tries to be Black/ Cause I talk with an accent, and grab on my balls/ So they always keep asking the same f**king questions/ What school did I go to, what hood I grew up in/ The why, the who, what, when, the where and the how/ 'til I'm grabbing my hair and I'm tearin' it out/ Cause they drivin' me crazy, I can't take it/ I'm racing, I'm pacing, I stand and I sit/ And I'm thankful for every fan that I get/ But I can't take a s**t in the bathroom without someone standing by it

Nicki Minaj in the song, *Dear Old Nicki* (2010) states:

Yo, did I chase the glitz and glamour, money, fame, and power?/ Cause if so, that will forever go down my lamest hour/ I should've kept you with me, gettin' at them nameless cowards/ They was no match for you, couldn't defeat your prowess/ I had to make them changes, I hoped you understood/ You see for every bad, I did a ton of good/ But you was underground, and I was mainstream/ I live the life now that we would daydream/ My only wish is you come enjoy it with me/ Get on them conference calls go meet the lawyers with me/ The money came yeah, tripled and quadrupled it/ But I still miss us when we was just on some stupid s**t/ And it's still f**k the media they ridiculed you/ never believed ya./ They just deaded you, left you in all black/ But dear old Nicki, please call back

J. Cole in the song, *Forest Hills Drive* (2014) states:

It's beauty in the struggle, ugliness in the success/ Hear my words or listen to my signal of distress/ I grew up in the city and though sometimes we had less/ Compared to some of my niggas down the block man we were blessed/ And life can't be no fairytale, no once upon a time/ But I be God damned if a nigga don't be tryin'.../ Cause pain still lingers on mine/ On the road to riches listen this is what you'll find/ The good news is nigga you came a long way/ The bad news is nigga you went the wrong way/ Think being broke was better

Despite which category one argues as being the most authentic part of Hip Hop's rap culture, both rappers continue to struggle, regardless of the choice to remain underground or change to become commercial. Underground artist struggle because of their choice to pursue passion over paychecks, while the commercial artist struggles because even though paychecks were chosen, there is an ongoing fight to preserve their passions, in spite of their actions.

Chapter 8

Hip Hop Culture Is Alive and Still Has a Voice for the Voiceless

July 1, 1982 marked an important day in Hip Hop culture; especially the rap culture, because the song *The Message*, by Grandmaster Flash and the Furious Five was released. *The Message (1982)* was a monumental song, because this was the first song that actually provided a realistic depiction, through the form of rap, about how real people were experiencing everyday life. When considering the timespan between 1982 and now, one must wonder how far has Hip Hop culture come and how far can the culture still go? The original intention of the culture was to provide a "message" to the world and be a "voice for the voiceless." The simple desire to speak for those who have no voice was a notable desire that has emerged far beyond what anyone could have imagined the culture to become.

Since the conception of *The Message* (1982), critics and

Hip Hop enthusiasts can agree on one singular fact, if nothing

else; Hip Hop culture; specifically rap has changed. Determining

whether the change is positive or negative depends on one's

current view of Hip Hop culture, as well an awareness of how Hip

Hop culture was before becoming a multi-billion dollar industry.

Many critics may believe that Hip Hop is nothing more than a

musical genre that degrades women, promotes promiscuity,

supports relational infidelity, encourages violence, and

egotistically brags of materialism. Critics and enthusiasts struggle

with evaluating the current messages in Hip Hop, because at

times the content of certain lyrics can appear contradictory and at

best indecisive and inconclusive. For example, one can hear a

song called, *How to Love (2011),* by Lil' Wayne that reveals a

deep desire to learn what love is and how to love a woman.

However, the genuine intentions of Lil' Wayne's words are

questioned, when one listens to other Lil' Wayne song lyrics, which are sexually provocative and includes constant references about genitals, sex acts, and drug references. In spite of the contradictions, artists should have the ability and freedom to express themselves (freely), just as the essence of African drum and dance encouraged people historically. Music and content should never be limited to a singular emotion, because as human beings we are not limited to a singular emotion or feeling.

Determining whether Hip Hop culture still has a relevant message, requires one to be knowledgeable about Hip Hop's history, connections to the past, and the other sub-genres of rap. Most people's perceptions about Hip Hop's culture are dictated by what is seen and heard. When it comes to understanding Hip Hop culture's history in its entirety, what is unseen and unheard is just as important as what is seen and heard. Music has always had an ability to unite people in ways that politics, religion, economics, generational gaps, and life cannot.

Common's 1994, song *I Used to Love H.E.R.* (Hearing. Every. Rhyme.) is an important representation of one's love towards a woman, metaphorically Hip Hop culture. Common's song, although criticized by other rappers (specifically rappers from the West Coast), identified the changes that relationships can go through, while subliminally describing the changes he has noticed is occurring in Hip Hop. Common's portrait of Hip Hop culture as female and not male, created a comparison between how men in Hip Hop treat women and the culture. Hip Hop culture was originally something that was once considered sacred, precious, attentive to the needs of the people, and relevant. Now, the culture appears to have changed and become secularized beyond originality, lyrically worthless, negligent, disrespectful, and ultimately irrelevant to the aspects of life that are most important.

Common may have expressed why he used to love her (aka Hip Hop) and why there appears to be a deterioration of that love, but Nas' declaration of *Hip Hop is Dead (2006)*, almost 12 years later, reveals the multi-dynamic issues that have destroyed Hip Hop. Nas' acclamations in the hook states, "Roll to every station, wreck the Dj," which explains how Dj's (the backbone of Hip Hop culture) have contributed to the death of Hip Hop culture. Dj's helped create, define, legitimize, and validate the sound of a culture; just as African drummers do in the ring circle. Unfortunately, the sound of Hip Hop culture is non-inspiring. For Nas, if Hip Hop is dead, then those who endorse fanciful imagery and linguistic coonery are partially to blame. Along with the Dj's are those who have diluted the culture by focusing on album sales and financial gain, rather than encouraging a healthy balance

between lyrical artistry and endorsing additional aspects of Hip
Hop culture, like graffiti, breakdancing, and beatboxing. For Nas,
the declaration of Hip Hop was not a permanent condemnation of
Hip Hop, but a deafening call out to those who participate and
love Hip Hop culture.

Today, additional concerns have increased about whether
Hip Hop culture's successful integration into pop culture has
diluted Hip Hop's message and ability to be a "voice for the
voiceless." Despite the controversial lyrics and the barrage of
questions surrounding Hip Hop culture's current message and
voice, one cannot deny how impactful the culture can be *when it
matters most* and when addressing issues like: politics, social
injustice, economic disparities, educational inequalities, violence,
and police brutality. Hip Hop culture; especially rappers, have
never shied away from controversy or idly sat by when blatant
injustice was occurring. In 1989, Krs-One, along with other

artists, started a Stop the Violence Movement, inspired by a song called, *Self-Destruction,* to address the on-going issue of Black-on-Black violence that was plaguing various communities. The song and movement provided a much-needed "message" and a "voice for the voiceless."

After the recent and controversial deaths involving police officers and Black people (specifically young Black men and women) like Sean Bell (killed 2006), Jordan Davis (killed 2012), Trayvon Martin (killed 2012), Jordan Davis (killed 2012), Michael Brown (killed 2014), Tamir Rice (killed 2014), Eric Garner (killed 2014), Walter Scott (killed 2015), Sandra Bland (killed 2015), Philando Castile (killed 2016), and Korryn Gaines (killed 2016), Hip Hop culture responded with a "message" and provided a "voice for the voiceless," just like Krs-One and others did in 1989. The 2014 song called, *Don't Shoot,* by The Game featuring various artists, reflected the thoughts and sentiments of many people, not just in America, but also worldwide. Deducing the historical or current impact of Hip Hop culture; specifically the art form of rap, would be diminishing the credibility of some of the most influential aspects and people in Hip Hop culture. As long as someone (from anywhere in the world) comes from nothing into something, while claiming, referencing, explaining, bragging, representing, and declaring their connection with Hip Hop culture, the founding pioneers and prominent contributors of Hip Hop culture **_will always_** have a redemptive message.

Chapter 9

Final Thoughts about Hip Hop: It Was, What It Was, For It Got

Here

Providing a final analysis of Hip Hop culture is difficult,
because the culture is ever growing. When accessing current Hip
Hop culture's influence on current day society; specifically
integration into popular culture, one would think Hip Hop has
finally arrived. Hip Hop culture has gained mass appeal and
acceptance in the most restrictive areas of the world. The
elements of Hip Hop culture; especially rap music has reached
places that most people do not even know exists. Hip Hop
culture's future was never fully imagined, when the movement
was first started. However, one should not be surprised to know
that some of the greatest leaders and Hip Hop powerhouses were

born during the post-Civil Rights era (Black Arts and Black

Panther Party Movements) specifically in the 1960's and 1970s:

Marlon Williams (Marley Marl), Stanley Kirk Burrell (MC
Hammer), William Michael Griffin Jr. (Rakim), Lawrence
Krisna Parker (Krs-One), Sean Carter (Jay-Z), Dana Owens
(Queen Latifah) Tupac Amaru Shakur (2Pac), Nasir Jones
(Nas), Earl Stevens (E-40), Members of EPMD (Erick
Sermon and Parrish Smith), Rahzel M. Brown (Rahzel),
Kimberly Jones (Lil' Kim) Christopher Wallace (Notorious
B.I.G.), Brad Terrence Jordan (Scarface), Bernard Freeman
(Bun B), André Lauren Benjamin (André 3000), Lana
Michele Mooorer (MC Lyte), James Todd Smith (LL Cool J),
Trevor Smith Jr. (Busta Rhymes), Inga DeCarlo Fung
Marchand (Foxy Brown), Earl Stevens (E-40), Marcel Theo
Hall (Biz Markie), Marshall Bruce Mathers III (Eminem),
Douglas E. Davis (Doug E. Fresh), Lonnie Rashid Lynne. Jr
(Common), Yolanda Whittaker (Yo-Yo), Calvin Broadus
(Snoop Dogg/Snoop Lion), Members of N.W.A.: Andre
Romelle Young (Dr.Dre), Eric Lynn Wright (Eazy-E), O'Shea
Jackson (Ice Cube), Mik Lezan (Arabian Prince), Lorenzo
Jerald Patterson (Mc Ren), and Antoine Carraby (Dj Yella),

Tracy Lauren Marrow (Ice T), Robin Yvette Allen (The Lady of Rage), Jason Phillips (Jadakiss), Christopher Rios (Big Pun), as well as members of Tribe Called Quest: Malik I. Taylor (Phife Dawg), Kamaal I.J. Fareed (Q-Tip), Jarobi White (Ali Shaheed), and lastly members of Wu Tang Clan: Robert Diggs (Rza), Dennis Cole (Ghostface Killer), Clifford Smith (Method Man), Russell T. Jones (Ol' Dirty Bastard), Corey Q. Woods (Raekwon), Gary Grice (GZA), Lamont J. Hawkins (U-God), Jason Hunter (Inspectah Deck), Jamel Irief (Masta Killa), and Darryl Hill (Cappadonna).

Each of these artists propelled Hip Hop culture into a worldwide phenomenon. In addition to those American born artists that impacted Hip Hop culture; are artists from other countries or small islands like:

Trinidad & Tobago (Onika Tanya Miraj aka Nicki Minaj), Kingston, Jamaica (Clive Campbell aka Dj Kool Herc), Bridgetown Barbados (Joseph Saddler aka Grandmaster Flash), Puerto Rico (Tego Calderón Rosario aka Tego) and

(Ramón Luis Ayala Rodríguez aka Daddy Yankee), or countries like Mitcham, London, United Kingdom (Richard Walters aka Slick Rick), Battersea, London, United Kingdom (Simone Gooden aka Monie Love), and Canada (Drake aka Aubrey "Drake" Graham).

The constant growth of Hip Hop culture within and outside of America reveals how influential a movement that started from the streets have popularized trends (nationally and internationally) and inspired an entire world.

Hip Hop Culture has gone through various stages of progression to reinvent the culture so that each generation (locally and globally) becomes familiar with Hip Hop culture. Hip Hop has been able to remain relevant with each generation by becoming multiculturally inclusive and incorporating multiple genres of music to create a new sound. Here are a few examples of how Hip Hop merged with:

- Rock to create Hip Hop Rock (example: Run DMC/Aerosmith's 1986 song, *Walk This Way*)
- Swing to create New Jack Swing (example: Guy's 1991 song, *New Jack City*)
- R&B to create Hip Hop R&B (example: Mary J. Blige & Method Man's 1995 song, *Your All I Need To Get By*)

Hip Hop's ability to evolve and reinvent to remain relevant has come with great success, but also great criticism. Unfortunately, Hip Hop culture has and often becomes overshadowed by continual negativity and violent imagery, degrading lyrics towards women, as well as reveal depictions inauthenticity, hyper-masculinity, and hyper-sexuality. Hip Hop's rawness has always been what has made the cultural movement authentic. Therefore, determining if authenticity is better revealed through positive imagery and lyricism over an over-promotion of negative harshness is based on personal opinion, rather than actualities. Just as Africans, in Africa, were entitled to freely express themselves through drumming and dancing (passively and aggressively) so should all aspects of Hip Hop culture. The fact that music is not a singular emotion is essential, because humans are not confined to a singular emotion.

Hip Hop culture was born to be controversial, just like the preceding historic movements. Public controversy sometimes has a better way of identifying issues than private conversations could ever do. Hip Hop culture's imperfections shows that the cultural is continual growing, because with each new generation that becomes exposed to the movement comes new mistakes and new lessons to be taught. Regardless of how one feels, those who were active in Hip Hop in the 1970s, passed the torch to those in the 1980s, and those in the 1980s, passed the torch to those in the 1990s, and so forth. With each generation, Hip Hop will either grow or die; but for now the culture continues to reflect and evolve in ways expected and un-expected.

List of References

Abrahams, Roger D. (1985). *African American Folktales: Stories of Black Traditions in the New World*. New York: Pantheon.

Aronson, Virginia. (2001). *The History of Motown*. Philadelphia: Chelsea House.

Bisson, Terry. (2005). *Nat Turner: Slave Revolt Leader*.Philadelphia: Chelsea House Publishers.

Black, Samuel. (2006). *The Harlem Renaissance Poets and Musicians*. TimBookTu. Retrieved from http://www.timbooktu.com/spence/harlem.htm.

Bradford, Sarah Hopkins (orig. pub. 1869), (1971). *Scenes in the Life of Harriet Tubman*. Freeport: Books for Libraries Press.

Churchill and Vander Wall (2002). *The COINTELPRO Papers: Documents from the FBI's Secret Wars Against Dissent in the United States*. South End Press.

CNN. (2008). *Tape shows woman dying on waiting room floor*. Retrieved from http://www.cnn.com/2008/US/07/01/waiting.room.death/indexhtml?eref=rs.

Emery, Andrew. (1997). *Schoolly D- Original Gangsta.* Retrieved from www.globaldarkness.com/articles/schooly_d_original_gangsta.htm

Gabbidon, S.L., & Greene, H.T. (2012). *Race and Crime (3rd edition)*. Thousand Oaks, CA: Sage Publications.

Johnson, A., & Johnson, R.(1979). *Propaganda and Aesthetics: The Literary Politics of Afro-American Magazines in the Twentieth Century*. Amherst: The University of Massachusetts Press, p.80-81.

Matthias, Blanche. (1923). Unknown Great Ones. The Woman Athletic.

Mosher, Donald L. and Serkin, M. (1984). Measuring a macho personality constellation. *Journal of Research in Personality*, 18 (2): 150-163.

Penrice, Ronda Racha. (2007). African American History for Dummies: Chapter 16: Give Me a Beat: African American Music. John Wiley & Songs, Inc. Hoboken, NJ. (p.309-315)

Rinehart, N.J. and McCabe, M.P. (1997). Hypersexuality: Psychopathology or normal variant of sexuality? *Sexual and Marital Therapy*, 45-60.

Smith, Jessie Carney. (2011). *Encyclopedia of African American Popular Culture*. Santa Barbara, California: Greenwood Press.

Strausbaugh, Jeremy P. (2006). *Black Like You: Blackface, Whiteface, Insult & Imitation in American Popular Culture*. Tarcher/Penguin Books.

Terres, John K. (1980). *Audubon Society Encyclopedia of North American Birds*. New York: Knopf. The Interactive Journal of Early American Life, Inc. (2001). *Common-Place*. Retrieved from http://www.common-place.org/vol-01/no-04/school/elkins.shtml

Van Deburg, William L. (1992). *New Day in Babylon: The Black Power Movement and American Culture, 1965-1975*. University of Chicago Press.

Whitaker, Matthew C. (2011). *Icons of Black America: Breaking Barriers and Crossing Boundaries, Volume 1*. Santa Barbara, California: ABC-CLIO, LLC. (p.693).

Index

A

Authenticity
    authentic, *iii*, *105*, *106*

B

B.I.G.
    Notorious, *8*, *48*, *97*, *110*, *123*
baby mama, *39*
breakdancing, *v*, *7*, *10*, *23*, *106*, *119*

C

clothing, *15*, *34*, *44*, *67*, *94*
commercial, *24*, *25*, *27*, *35*, *98*, *110*
    commercially, *26*, *97*, *109*, *110*, *113*
Common, *31*, *83*, *117*, *118*, *123*, *133*

D

Dark Alliance, *42*
dj'ing, *10*, *16*, *18*, *21*, *22*, *106*
drugs, *25*, *41*, *42*, *44*, *47*, *59*, *63*, *67*, *76*, *85*, *108*

F

female rapper, *60*, *93*, *94*, *95*, *96*, *100*, *101*, *102*, *104*

G

guns, *59*, *63*, *82*

H

hyper-masculine, *58*
hyper-sexual, *58*

CPSIA information can be obtained
at www.ICGtesting.com
Printed in the USA
BVOW08s0816080917
494273BV00001B/29/P